LETTERS FROM CHRIST

A COMPILATION OF WORDS FROM CHRIST TO YOU

Yaeli Popovici

Letters from Christ: A Compilation Of Words From Christ To You
Copyright © 2018 Yaeli Popovici

All rights reserved. No part of this book may be used or reproduced by any means, graphic, electronic, mechanical, including photocopying, recording, taping, or by any information storage retrieval system without the written permission of the author except in the case of brief quotations embodied in critical articles and reviews.

Scripture quotations taken from the **NASB**. Copyright by The Lockman Foundation. (www.lockman.org.)

ISBN: 978-1717434142
ISBN-13: 1717434142

LOC Control Number: 2018942870

Pulpit to Page Publishing Co. books may be ordered through booksellers or by contacting:
Pulpit to Page Publishing Co.
Warsaw, Indiana
pulpittopage.com

PULPITTOPAGE.COM
U.S.A. & ABROAD

A NOTE FROM THE AUTHOR

Dear Reader,

This book is a compilation of words that Christ spoke to me, so that I could pass them along to you. This book is not my own but Christ's, I am merely a servant of Him. As you read, you'll see an individual letter from Christ, along with a corresponding verse of Scripture, and a brief thought from me.

I hope this book inspires you to just sit down and listen to what He wants to tell you. I encourage you to read through these slowly and take your time to listen to what Jesus wants to speak to you through this, and what He has written to me so I can tell you.

— Yaeli Popovici

Yaeli Popovici

| Letter 1 |

I am your God, I am your love. I am the one who saves you from the pit of despair. Oh child, it is the God of David and Abraham that speaks to you. I am the one who saved you from captivity. I broke off your chains. I kissed your feet. I brought you up to solid ground and lavishly clothed you in wisdom and righteousness.

—Your Love

"And there is salvation in no one else; for there is no other name under heaven that has been given among men by which we must be saved."
—*Acts 4:12*

God cannot just leave us alone. He cannot resist coming to us with his arms open wide.

| Letter 2 |

I've given you water to fill your stomach but My living water will fill you eternally. I have given you a family but you also have a family in Me. I have given you the gift of love but my love is greater than all. Be obedient and have wisdom for behold you live in a world full of sin yet we found each other.

—The Living Water

"But to each one of us grace was given according to the measure of Christ's gift."

—*Ephesians 4:7*

He is enough for me but I just can't get enough of Him.

| Letter 3 |

I died for you so I could cherish you. I laid my life down so you could hear my voice. I allowed my body to be broken because I wanted you to know I love you. You are my sweet joy and love's child. It is my honor to die for you. Let it be yours.

—Broken One

"He was despised and forsaken of men, A man of sorrows and acquainted with grief; And like one from whom men hide their face He was despised, and we did not esteem Him. Surely our griefs He Himself bore, And our sorrows He carried; Yet we ourselves esteemed Him stricken, Smitten of God, and afflicted. But He was pierced through for our transgressions, He was crushed for our iniquities; The chastening for our well-being fell upon Him, And by His scourging we are healed."

—*Isaiah 53:3-5*

The Son of God didn't just pay our ransom. He was our ransom, paying with His own body.

| Letter 4 |

Even if your sacrifices are as numerous as the stars don't forget I will never leave you. Even when you are feeling weak and your hope is wavering, don't forget I will never leave you. Even when you doubt me and sin don't forget I will never leave you. When you feel like you can't make it, don't forget I have a hold of your hand like you have a hold on my heart.

—The Sacrifice

"'Do not fear, for I am with you; do not anxiously look about you, for I am your God. I will strengthen you, surely I will help you, Surely I will uphold you with My righteous right hand."

—Isaiah 41:10

God is always there, it's our responsibility to pay attention to Him.

| Letter 5 |

Show the world My joy. Bring My light and life to the grieving, dying, depressed world in which my beloved people live.

—The Light

"And He said to them, "Go into all the world and preach the gospel to all creation."

—Mark 16:15

The world will never again see a sacrifice as great as Jesus, yet still how many millions do not believe in this sacrifice.

| Letter 6 |

I am your only true Savior. May I be the only think you think about. I want to be your obsession and captor of your heart. Be forever mine, dear beloved, be captivated by My beauty. I will be your prized possession and you will be mine.

—Father

"He predestined us to adoption as sons through Jesus Christ to Himself, according to the kind intention of His will."

—*Ephesians 1:5*

The moment Christ becomes our obsession and we allow Him to come and completely takeover is the moment all spiritual boundaries can be broken.

| Letter 7 |

It is under the shadow of My wings where you will find complete rest. The world is dangerous so run to Me. It has been made dangerous by those who fell. They reflected themselves throughout the earth and eagerly await the dying sinner. Listen to My words and heed My instruction.

—Comforter

"So also is the resurrection of the dead. It is sown a perishable body, it is raised an imperishable body; it is sown in dishonor, it is raised in glory; it is sown in weakness, it is raised in power; it is sown a natural body, it is raised a spiritual body. If there is a natural body, there is also a spiritual body."

—1 Corinthians 15:42-44

| Letter 8 |

You are a tree planted in My garden. My love for you is eternal. I want to be with you always so I gave you a way to communicate. I have given you the Holy Spirit. My love for you goes wild and I sit and wait for you to speak. It takes away my grief when I talk to my people.

—The Vine Dresser

"Also I will restore the captivity of My people Israel, And they will rebuild the ruined cities and live in them; They will also plant vineyards and drink their wine, and make gardens and eat their fruit."

—Amos 9:14

No one can reach the endless, immeasurable bottom of Jesus' sacrificial love because there is no bottom.

| Letter 9 |

People of the world you are weak and sick in the soul. Your spirits are dead. Light cannot enter you; hurry and repent. Am I not the Redeemer? Have I not already saved you? Believe in Me and I will set you free. My compassion for you is unending and My want for you goes on. No matter how many sins you have I will wash you by hand and give you my heart.

—Redeemer

"He has sent redemption to His people; He has ordained His covenant forever; Holy and awesome is His name."

—*Psalm 111:9*

The day the sinner acknowledges his Savior and lifts Him up as his most prized possession is the day that heaven gets closer to earth.

Yaeli Popovici

| Letter 10 |

I love you. You are a gem in my holy crown and a sparkle in my robe. I will protect you always, even when you think you are strong. I will always love you. You are a cherished thing in My sight. A lamb that was found. You belong to Me, oh beautiful child. Speak to me as I speak to you. I want all your love for Me.

—Holy Protector

"I am my beloved's and my beloved is mine, He who pastures his flock among the lilies."

—*Song of Solomon 6:3*

The love of the sacrificial Lamb is irreplaceable and was given with sweet humility.

| Letter 11 |

Oh people, how I love you. I yearn to be loved back by you. Don't be afraid to follow and share Christ. Oh people, you do not know the way I grieve for you. I am saddened by your blindness. If only you'd see Me. I have died for you. I took away your pain, sickness, depression and sin. Now please I ask, come find Me. I am right in front of you.

—The Savior

"Wash me thoroughly from my iniquity And cleanse me from my sin."

—*Psalm 51:2*

"This is good and acceptable in the sight of God our Savior, who desires all men to be saved and to come to the knowledge of the truth."

—*1 Timothy 2:3-4*

It was the only innocent blameless person in the world who took on the sins of the world and died.

| Letter 12 |

My dear sheep, don't shy away. Love Me. Don't wander to see the gifts beyond. Truly I say, those gifts are fake. You are with the greatest gift of all — Me. When you stumble I will lift you up on My shoulders. I will make sure that you're fine. I shall be known as a humble, lowly Shepherd who loves
His sheep.

—The Greatest Gift of All

"Like a shepherd He will tend His flock, In His arm He will gather the lambs And carry them in His bosom; He will gently lead the nursing ewes."

—*Isaiah 40:11*

"And when the Chief Shepherd appears, you will receive the unfading crown of glory."

—*1 Peter 5:4*

And this broken body and innocent soul is the greatest gift of all.

| Letter 13 |

You were made like Me. You were made by Me. You were made for Me. Take pleasure in Me as I take pleasure in you. Together we are united. We are one in love. I lifted you above the storm and laid you on a solid rock. Seek only Me. Want only Me. Give your whole self over to be baptized in the fire of my love and My sweet presence.

—The Maker

"Beloved, now we are children of God, and it has not appeared as yet what we will be. We know that when He appears, we will be like Him, because we will see Him just as He is."

—1 John 3:2

When you seek and want only the Lord you become unmoved by the devil's works.

| Letter 14 |

It is My name that heals, My love that redeems, My death that brings life, My justice that saves, My people I've created. Call out and I'll save you, my beloved. You are amazing in My sight.

—The Just King

"For this reason also, God highly exalted Him, and bestowed on Him the name which is above every name, so that at the name of Jesus every knee will bow, of those who are in heaven and on earth and under the earth, and that every tongue will confess that Jesus Christ is Lord, to the glory of God the Father."

—*Philippians 2:9-11*

Self-denial is one of the most Christ-like acts we can acquire.

| Letter 15 |

I will lift you up in My arms and carry you home. I will cleanse you in clear water and wash off your dirt. Holding you in My tender arms I'll dress your wound and provide you with nourishment. I will speak loving words to you and caress your face with My hands. I have finally found one of My lost children. You are an orphan no longer, I will never let go.

—Jesus the Servant

"And do not be conformed to this world, but be transformed by the renewing of your mind, so that you may prove what the will of God is, that which is good and acceptable and perfect."

—Romans 12:2

"Create in me a clean heart, O God, And renew a steadfast spirit within me."

—Psalm 51:10

His loving reflection shows us how dirty and broken we really are.

| Letter 16 |

I shall search everywhere for you. No matter what I shall not stop til I find you. When I find you I will rejoice; the angels will sing praises. They shall gladly play their harps and sing with all their might. Truly I say the heavens will rejoice when a sheep is returned to its flock.

—The Loving Shepherd

"My people have become lost sheep; Their shepherds have led them astray. They have made them turn aside on the mountains; They have gone along from mountain to hill and have forgotten their resting place."

—*Jeremiah 50:6*

"Know that the Lord Himself is God; It is He who has made us, and not we ourselves; We are His people and the sheep of His pasture."

—*Psalm 100:3*

It is unlike God's nature to ever stop searching.

| Letter 17 |

My sweet creation, I rejoice in My work. Abound in My love. This everlasting love that comes from My well that will never run dry. My sweet creation, look how I shaped and molded you. Appreciate the work of My hands. These are the same hands that were nailed to the cross.

—Lord of lords

"Do all things without grumbling or disputing."

—*Philippians 2:14*

We should do all things without grumbling, and if spending time with Jesus is like a chore to us then may we immediately be rebuked for our deep selfishness.

| Letter 18 |

I am the lover of your soul. Won't you let me love you? Why don't you turn around and look at Me? What do you fear? Is it so hard to obey? So hard to listen? So hard to wait? Do you feel like I owe you for your time? Oh people, I gave you your time, as well as your life.

—Heaven's Ruler

"You have granted me life and lovingkindness; And Your care has preserved my spirit."

—Job 10:12

"The Spirit of God has made me, and the breath of the Almighty gives me life."

—Job 33:4

| Letter 19 |

My beloved, sweet people: worship Me. I have set you free from the cross. I've died for you. Praise Me as long as you live. Think of Me all of the time. Speak My words all the time. Don't forget about Me. Don't go on ahead without Me. Wait and have patience. We will go together hand in hand.

—Chain Breaker

"He predestined us to adoption as sons through Jesus Christ to Himself, according to the kind intention of His will."

—*Ephesians 1:5*

Thank Him, praise Him, breathe Him, need Him.

| Letter 20 |

I have given My people in the wilderness bread and water. Will I not also provide for you? Do not be afraid I say, I will make sure you are okay. You are safe in the shadow of My glorious wings. They will give you rest. Lie down and drink from Me for behold, you belong to Me.

—Provider

"And my God will supply all your needs according to His riches in glory in Christ Jesus."
—*Philippians 4:19*

"I, the Lord, am your God, who brought you up from the land of Egypt; Open your mouth wide and I will fill it."
—*Psalm 81:10*

Provision is always available to the humble.

| Letter 21 |

Take heart and do not lose hope. Have patience to hear what I have to say next. Take up the gifts of wisdom and righteousness. In humility worship Me. Do not boast of anything but Me. Take heed, I want to dwell in your heart. Keep it clean before Me and do not defile your hole temple. For I say, truly then the kingdom of heaven belongs to you.

—Patient One

"For God, who said, 'Light shall shine out of darkness,' is the One who has shone in our hearts to give the Light of the knowledge of the glory of God in the face of Christ. But we have this treasure in earthen vessels, so that the surpassing greatness of the power will be of God and not from ourselves."
—*2 Corinthians 4:6-7*

"But when God, who had set me apart even from my mother's womb and called me through His grace, was pleased to reveal His Son in me so that I might preach Him among the Gentiles, I did not immediately consult with flesh and blood."
—*Galatians 1:15-16*

If I could ever do something that would cause Jesus to forever leave me, then may my heart also leave me for I could not live for a second without Him.

| Letter 22 |

Only in Me you can find complete rest. Under My wings you can finally be content. Why are you hesitant to come to Me? Don't be. Run as fast as you can towards My arms. Find happiness and joy in the bliss of My person.

—Giver of Rest

"Come to Me, all who are weary and heavy-laden, and I will give you rest. Take My yoke upon you and learn from Me, for I am gentle and humble in heart, and you will find rest for your souls. For My yoke is easy and My burden is light."
—Matthew 11:28-30

Without Jesus I am mere dust, with Him I am a child of God in heaven.

| Letter 23 |

Child, do not cower to fear. Do not let fear of loss control you. Stand up in boldness, rebuke that of the devil. Speak of your faith, don't be afraid of persecution. Dear little one, am I not right here? Are you not doing it for My sake? I could never leave those I love. Speak out directly against evil with abounding faith and love on fire for Me.

—The Fire

"What then shall we say to these things? If God is for us, who is against us?"

—Romans 8:31

"This was in accordance with the eternal purpose which He carried out in Christ Jesus our Lord, in whom we have boldness and confident access through fait in Him."

—Ephesians 3:11-12

Enduring persecution is hopeless if you don't know who you're enduring it for. So know that it is unto the Lord and wear your scars proudly just as He had.

| Letter 24 |

Speak My name throughout the whole world. Do not stop there. Tell the rich and poor, strong and weak. Remind the Christian and tell the non-Christian. Remind them of Me. May My words cause their deaf ears to be open so they will be lifted up towards me.

—The Good News

"Go therefore and make disciples of all the nations, baptizing them in the name of the Father and the Son and the Holy Spirit, teaching them to observe all that I commanded you; and lo, I am with you always, even to the end of the age."

—*Matthew 28:19-20*

If we need prayer then those who are lost need prayer one hundred thousand times more than we do because they do not know the name of Jesus Christ who saves.

| Letter 25 |

There is not an ounce of sin found in My Son. In all His ways He is perfect. Nor will you find defilement or slyness of His heart. He will never deceive or lie. Only good things come from my Son. He has made a covenant with man, He will not go back on His word. My people will be saved in the last days.

—The Perfect Son

"You know that He appeared in order to take away sins; and in Him there is no sin."

—*1 John 3:5*

"For we do not have a high priest who cannot sympathize with our weaknesses, but One who has been tempted in all things as we are, yet without sin."

—*Hebrews 4:15*

| Letter 26 |

It was on the cross that I took on pain for you. I felt guilt. I felt loneliness without my Father for I am always with Him. My body was pierced and beaten. My soul felt heavy from sin - all the sin I took up. I hung there with tears, my heart was broken for those who beat me. For the lonely, for the fatherless orphans all around me. Now let me tell you, you are an orphan no longer.

—The Crucificial Lamb

"For while we were still helpless, at the right time Christ died for the ungodly."
—Romans 5:6

"For Christ also died for sins once for all, the just for the unjust, so that He might bring us to God, having been put to death in the flesh, but made alive in the spirit."
—1 Peter 3:18

I am dirty, He is clean. I am charged guilty, He is deemed innocent. I am wicked, He is blameless. I am sinful, He is pure. I lived, He died. I killed Him, He loved me.

| Letter 27 |

I am the King of the Jews. I love My people. Don't doubt My words. I wore My crown of thorns with much grief and compassion for My people. For still they do not know. Tell My people: I will heal blind eyes and bring hearing to those with ears that cannot hear. I can do anything. Have faith.

—The King of the Jews

"And above His head they put up the charge against Him [a]which read, 'THIS IS JESUS THE KING OF THE JEWS.'"

—*Matthew 27:37*

"To open blind eyes, To bring out prisoners from the dungeon And those who dwell in darkness from the prison."

—*Isaiah 42:7*

None of us love the wicked fool but Jesus died for billions of them.

| Letter 28 |

I reign. I am the ruler of heaven and of earth. People shall see Me and be in holy fear. I through My people will bring floods of peace, restoration and godly love to this barren land you live in. So many don't have My love. So many don't know Me. I have given My people the responsibility of sharing Christ and My nature. Take up your crosses and follow Me.

—The Ruler of Heaven

"For the Son of Man has come to seek and to save that which was lost."

—*Luke 19:10*

This land was made to be fruitful. Where is the fruit? Look at what sin has done to this once beautiful world.

| Letter 29 |

Even when time are hard, remember Me and what I did for you. Also when there are times of wealth and prosperity, remember Me and don't let your pride be even greater than it is. I want to see you like Me... like a Father and a child of the kingdom.

—Prince of Peace

"That they should put their confidence in God and not forget the works of God, But keep His commandments."
—*Psalm 78:7*

It's so easy to forget things and where they come from. So remember Jesus night and day, minute by minute, second by second.

| Letter 30 |

My son, My daughter, do not sit and worry. Do not fear. I love you. I promise I always will. You are the one I have chosen. Especially written for you at this time so you would not lose hope and forget Me. But may this just make you stronger and bolder. Seek wisdom when making decisions and don't take My good works lightly. I love you.

—Wise Father

"But You, O Lord, are a shield about me, My glory, and the One who lifts my head. I was crying to the Lord with my voice, and He answered me from His holy mountain. Selah. I lay down and slept; I awoke, for the Lord sustains me. I will not be afraid of ten thousands of people who have set themselves against me round about."

—Psalm 3:3-6

Fear is the devil's greatest weapon. Jesus beat it. We've beat it one hundred thousand times by staying courageous in the Lord, so why are you still scared?

| Letter 31 |

Every time you pray, you fast, you wait upon Me, you speak to Me, you claim your love to Me, you worship Me. You act in service for another and you are obedient. Truly I tell you at that time you have truly touched the heart of Jesus. My mercy is refreshing and My grace is forever. Remember Me, My people.

—Seeker

"With all prayer and petition pray at all times in the Spirit, and with this in view, be on the alert with all perseverance and petition for all the saints."

—*Ephesians 6:18*

Keeping close to Jesus is the secret to life and success.

| Letter 32 |

The moment you were born, I loved you. The moment you found Me, I rejoiced! For I had waited and you had finally come to Me. Never go back. Stay faithful and be fruitful. Preach to My people. Teach them My Word. For I love them too.

—Abounding Love

"Therefore the Lord longs to be gracious to you, and therefore He waits on high to have compassion on you. For the Lord is a God of justice; how blessed are all those who long for Him."

—Isaiah 30:18

We were loved before we knew what love was.

| Letter 33 |

Christ strengthens, Christ saves, Christ loves, Christ breaks down the old and evil and builds up the new and glorious. Christ is in a family. Christ died for us. Christ seeks your attention. Be attentive to the Most High.

—Christ

"Yet those who wait for the Lord will gain new strength; they will mount up with wings like eagles, they will run and not get tired, they will walk and not become weary."

—Isaiah 40:31

He is my all, He has all access.

| Letter 34 |

My love is deeper than the ocean floor and more wild than the rushing waves. Its currents will take you deeper into such a tangible love you could never imagine. I want that love to flood the earth and to fill the lost and strengthen My weary people. Open your eyes and see My love. It is unique. There is nothing like it. Come and enter it.

—Love

"Give thanks to the God of heaven, For His lovingkindness is everlasting."

—*Psalm 136:26*

May His love flood this dry land and fill dreary hearts.

| Letter 35 |

When the time comes for you to walk on water I'll be there holding My hand out, waiting for you to join Me. When the time comes for you to pass through the flames of a burning fire, I'll be there to walk through with you. I am the all-consuming fire — nothing can stop Me. Walk with Me in reassurance.

—All Consuming Fire

"Be strong and courageous, do not be afraid or tremble at them, for the Lord your God is the one who goes with you. He will not fail you or forsake you."

—*Deuteronomy 31:6*

"No man will be able to stand before you all the days of your life. Just as I have been with Moses, I will be with you; I will not fail you or forsake you."

—*Joshua 1:5*

| Letter 36 |

Those who truly love Me with all their hearts will be rewarded in heaven by My Father. Those who cry out to Me, I will listen to. Speak without doubt but with faith and your prayer shall come to pass. Don't take the Lord lightly, I am the most holy sacrifice to this world. Stay in My presence at all times.

—The Lord

"I press on toward the goal for the prize of the upward call of God in Christ Jesus."

—*Philippians 3:14*

"Now faith is the assurance of things hoped for, the conviction of things not seen."

—*Hebrews 11:1*

| Letter 37 |

My thoughts of you are more than sand. They are more precious than rubies and more valuable than diamonds. Surely I tell you, you are always on the mind of God. I am in love with you, My followers. Come and experience My beauty. I think you are special.

—The Cornerstone

"Your eyes have seen my unformed substance; and in Your book were all written the days that were ordained for me, when as yet there was not one of them. How precious also are Your thoughts to me, O God! How vast is the sum of them!"
—Psalm 139:16-17

The best medicine for the soul is to know Jesus and that He cares.

| Letter 38 |

I made the endless sky and the very deep oceans. I created land that is dry, the creation of flourishing trees and plants are Mine. I created all. You live in the artwork of God and you are My masterpiece. I love what I have made. Nature, animals, people alike. You were created in My image.

—Creator

"For we are His workmanship, created in Christ Jesus for good works, which God prepared beforehand so that we would walk in them."

—Ephesians 2:10

"For every house is built by someone, but the builder of all things is God."

—Hebrews 3:4

Allow God to put His paintbrush on the blank canvas of your heart and just paint.

| Letter 39 |

I will forever stay faithful. I'll never be far away. I am always with you even if you don't feel My presence. I love to see you. My grace is eternal and My real presence is powerful. I am the Almighty and the Most High. Hear My words as I speak.

—Faithful Father

"The Lord your God is in your midst, A victorious warrior. He will exult over you with joy, He will be quiet in His love, He will rejoice over you with shouts of joy."
—*Zephaniah 3:17*

"…teaching them to observe all that I commanded you; and lo, I am with you always, even to the end of the age."
—*Matthew 28:20*

It is when you're in the presence of Jesus that you realize how weak you really are and how much help you need to get back on your feet.

| Letter 40 |

Keep wanting Me. Keep getting to know Me. Keep running after Me. Keep loving Me. Never be satisfied with some of Me, but want all of Me. I love you.

—I AM

"Then Jesus said to His disciples, 'If anyone wishes to come after Me, he must deny himself, and take up his cross and follow Me.'"

—*Matthew 16:24*

Never be satisfied with *some* of him but want *all* of him.

| Letter 41 |

The mountains are My footstool, the flowers carry My fragrant aroma. I have made nature in My likeness. The sky is My throne, the ocean waves are My steps. My love is more dangerous than a fire, more strong than the ocean's current and more passionate than the whirling of the wind. It is eternal.

—Wonder Worker

"In whose hand are the depths of the earth, the peaks of the mountains are His also. The sea is His, for it was He who made it, and His hands formed the dry land."

—*Psalm 95:4-5*

| Letter 42 |

Though you sleep I never do. I watch over you. My angels protect you. When you are awake and thinking of different things, I am thinking of you. I sit down to watch the children play. Have innocence like a child. A child needs a caretaker to survive. Let Me be your caretaker as well as your friend.

—Caretaker

"But the Lord is faithful, and He will strengthen and protect you from the evil one."

—*2 Thessalonians 3:3*

"He will not allow your foot to slip; He who keeps you will not slumber."

—*Psalm 121:3*

The Lord's mind is always on His children. Only those that become like a child can enter the kingdom of God.

| Letter 43 |

I love, I save, I come to move and work in My people, to reveal who I am, to manifest and burn in hearts. I come to speak, to show up, and to love them and bring My ultimate everlasting power.

—Tower of Fortress

"Do not think that I came to abolish the Law or the Prophets; I did not come to abolish but to fulfill."
—Matthew 5:17

The mission of Jesus Christ was to take a hold of you and never let go. As children of the kingdom, it is also our responsibility to speak to the lost and help allow Jesus in their lives.

| Letter 44 |

Dear people, don't grow faint and lose hope, thinking that I shall not come in the last days, and I shall not feed My sheep. Don't doubt that I will fulfill My promises. I will when the time is right. I will not forget you or what I have said. I care about you.

—Promiser

"Consider it all joy, my brethren, when you encounter various trials, knowing that the testing of your faith produces endurance. And let endurance have its perfect result, so that you may be perfect and complete, lacking in nothing."

—James 1:2-4

Just because they lost their way does not mean that God forgot about them.

| Letter 45 |

Pray for the lost. My people who have strayed thinking they found a better way. I love them all the same. Their ways I despise but I still desire for their souls to be saved. I cannot help it. Pray earnestly for the lost to see Me. Spread the good news of My presence and eternal life in Me.

—Lover of the Lost

"Brethren, my heart's desire and my prayer to God for them is for their salvation."

—Romans 10:1

"…to open their eyes so that they may turn from darkness to light and from the dominion of Satan to God, that they may receive forgiveness of sins and an inheritance among those who have been sanctified by faith in Me."

—Acts 26:18

Jesus cannot help but fall in love with man. He cannot pull himself away from them. May the love of God burn in our hearts so we would be willing to reach the lost at any cost for His sake.

| Letter 46 |

I love when My people repent and give their life over to Me. I want to tear down the wall between us with My hands. I long for My people to leave their sinful lives and live in Me. I want to hold them in My hands and wash their worn feet and heal their bruised bodies. Please, please come. Return to Me.

—Sinless One

"Therefore repent and return, so that your sins may be wiped away, in order that times of refreshing may come from the presence of the Lord."

—*Acts 3:19*

"He has sent redemption to His people; He has ordained His covenant forever; Holy and awesome is His name."

—*Psalm 111:9*

"Let the redeemed of the Lord say so, whom He has redeemed from the hand of the adversary."

—*Psalm 107:2*

How many other kings care about their people like this King does?

| Letter 47 |

To My followers, be a bright light in this dark world. Be a humble example in this proud world. Be a lowly servant of Christ in this lavish, selfish world. Be a lover of Me in a self-loving world. I love you. Don't hold onto this makeshift world. Don't want *things* more than eternity. This would be vain. Enjoy life without idolizing it.

—Lowly Servant

"Be imitators of me, just as I also am of Christ."

—1 Corinthians 11:1

"…nor yet as lording it over those allotted to your charge, but proving to be examples to the flock."

—1 Peter 5:3

"Be diligent to present yourself approved to God as a workman who does not need to be ashamed, accurately handling the word of truth."

—2 Timothy 2:15

Be how Jesus was… how no one expected Him… a loyal servant-like lover of His Father.

| Letter 48 |

Choose Me before those who choose the world and be bold in faith. I love even those who don't love Me, who hate Me, who shun Me, and who defile My holy name. I love those who have never even heard the name Jesus. My heart longs for theirs. Cry out, oh broken hearts!

—Lover of Your Soul

"Set your mind on the things above, not on the things that are on earth."

—*Colossians 3:2*

| Letter 49 |

I want to share everything with you. Rest in My presence and drink from My communion.

—Sharer of Life

"But I say to you, love your enemies and pray for those who persecute you."

—*Matthew 5:44*

God doesn't want you to pick another cup from the table. He wants you to choose His and drink from it.

| Letter 50 |

I am your Father and your Victory. I help you overcome the darkness trapped inside the edges of your heart. Run to Me, run to Me, you are now a freed captive. Now go help free the captives. And only in My name, speak.

—Victory

"The Spirit of the Lord God is upon me, because the Lord has anointed me to bring good news to the afflicted; He has sent me to bind up the brokenhearted, to proclaim liberty to captives and freedom to prisoners."

—Isaiah 61:1

"So now, I will break his yoke bar from upon you, and I will tear off your shackles."

—Nahum 1:13

Dedicate all you do to Christ, for the victory is ours.

LETTERS FROM CHRIST

YAELI POPOVICI

PULPITTOPAGE.COM
U.S.A. & ABROAD

Yaeli Popovici

Letters from Christ:
A Compilation Of Words From Christ To You
Copyright © 2018 Yaeli Popovici